Tyrannosaurus Rex
Lori Dittmer

CREATIVE EDUCATION
CREATIVE PAPERBACKS

seedlings

Published by Creative Education and Creative Paperbacks
P.O. Box 227, Mankato, Minnesota 56002
Creative Education and Creative Paperbacks
are imprints of The Creative Company
www.thecreativecompany.us

Design by Ellen Huber
Production by Rachel Klimpel and Ciara Beitlich
Art direction by Rita Marshall

Photographs by Alamy (Science Photo Library, Stocktrek Images, Inc.),
Corbis (Bettman), Dreamstime (leonello calvetti), Getty (DE AGOSTINI
PICTURE LIBRARY, Mark Stevenson/Stocktrek Images), iStock
(Grassetto, kutaytinar), Science Source (CLAUS LUNAU / SCIENCE
PHOTO LIBRARY), Shutterstock (Ton Bangkeaw, Catmando, Herschel
Hoffmeyer, SciePro, Warpaint)

Library of Congress Cataloging-in-Publication Data
Names: Dittmer, Lori, author.
Title: Tyrannosaurus rex / by Lori Dittmer.
Description: Mankato, Minnesota : Creative Education and Creative
    Paperbacks, [2024] | Series: Seedlings: dinosaurs | Includes
    bibliographical references and index. | Audience: Ages 4–7 |
    Audience: Grades K–1 | Summary: "Early readers are introduced
    to Tyrannosaurus rex, a ferocious carnivore of the late Cretaceous
    period. Friendly text and dynamic photos share the dinosaur's looks,
    behaviors, and diet, based on scientific research"— Provided by
    publisher.
Identifiers: LCCN 2022015669 (print) | LCCN 2022015670 (ebook) | ISBN
    9781640265066 (library binding) | ISBN 9781682770580 (paperback) |
    ISBN 9781640006362 (ebook)
Subjects: LCSH: Tyrannosaurus rex—Juvenile literature. | Dinosaurs—
    Juvenile literature.
Classification: LCC QE862.S3 D587 2024 (print) | LCC QE862.S3 (ebook) |
    DDC 567.912/9—dc23/eng20221202
LC record available at https://lccn.loc.gov/2022015669
LC ebook record available at https://lccn.loc.gov/2022015670

Printed in China

TABLE OF CONTENTS

Hello,
Tyrannosaurus rex!

This dinosaur lived long ago.

Triceratops and *Ankylosaurus* lived at the same time.

***Tyrannosaurus rex* fossils** **were first found in 1902 by Barnum Brown.**

This dinosaur's name means "tyrant lizard king."

T. rex stomped on two feet. It was about as tall as two refrigerators.

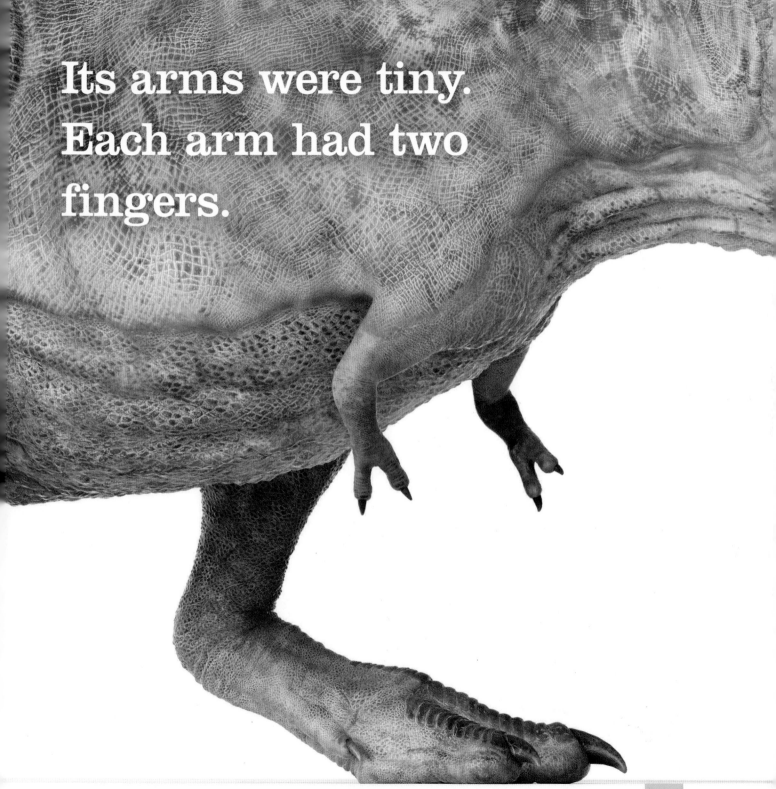

Its arms were tiny.
Each arm had two
fingers.

A thick neck held up its huge head. About 60 long teeth filled its mouth.

Each sharp tooth was as big as a banana.

T. rex tooth

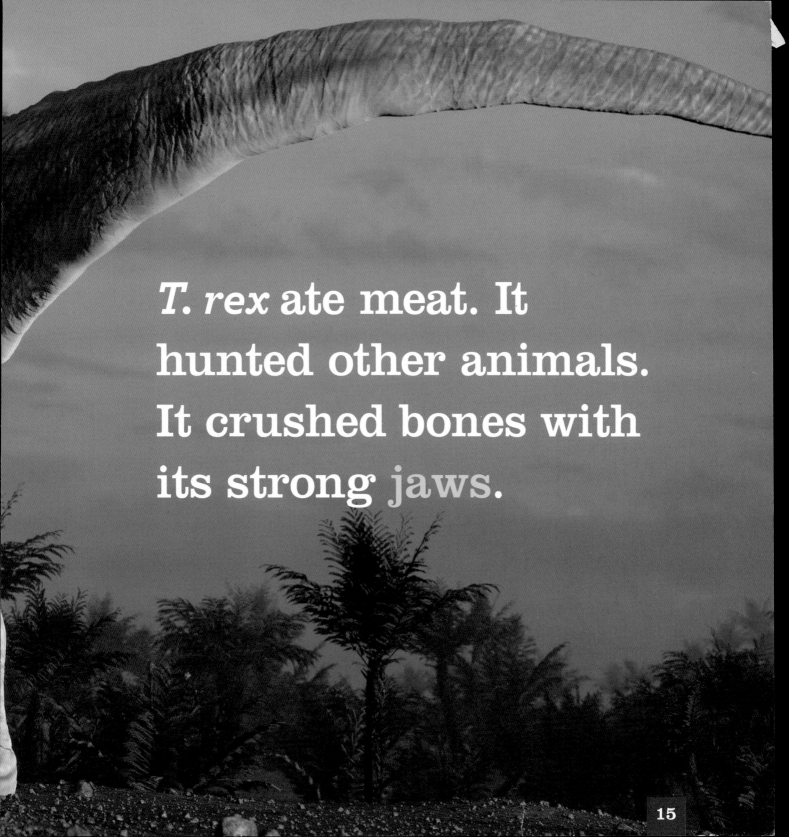

T. rex ate meat. It hunted other animals. It crushed bones with its strong jaws.

T. rex smelled the air.

It looked for food.

It was always hungry!

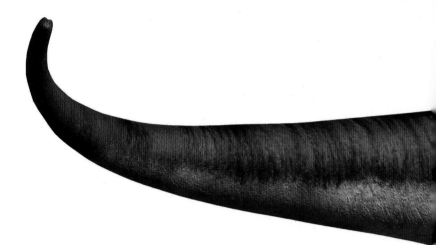

Goodbye, *Tyrannosaurus rex!*

Picture a *Tyrannosaurus rex*

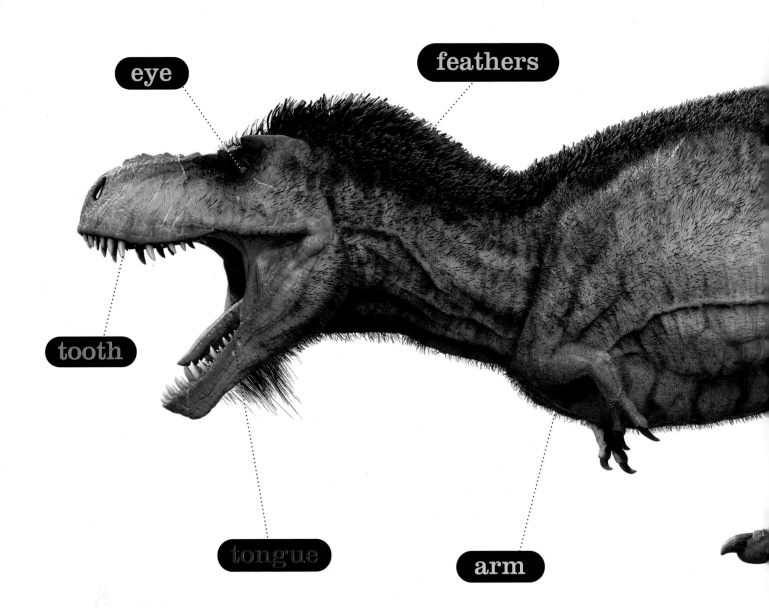

eye

feathers

tooth

tongue

arm

tail

leg

claw

Words to Know

fossil: a bone or trace from an animal long ago that can be found in some rocks

jaw: the bony part of the mouth that holds teeth

tyrant: a cruel ruler

Read More

Eason, Sarah. *Bones in the Cliff: T. Rex Discovery*. Minneapolis: Bearport Publishing, 2022.

Kaiser, Brianna. *The Mighty T. Rex*. Minneapolis: Lerner Publications, 2022.

Websites

American Museum of Natural History | PaleontOLogy
https://www.amnh.org/explore/ology/paleontology
Read stories, play games, and watch videos.

National Geographic Kids | *Tyrannosaurus Rex*
https://kids.nationalgeographic.com/animals/prehistoric-animals/tyrannosaurus-rex
Read more about *Tyrannosaurus rex* and watch a video.

Note: Every effort has been made to ensure that the websites listed above are suitable for children, that they have educational value, and that they contain no inappropriate material. However, because of the nature of the Internet, it is impossible to guarantee that these sites will remain active indefinitely or that their contents will not be altered.

Index